Overcome Trauma

I0625441

A Comprehensive Guide to Understanding, Healing and Moving Forward from Past Trauma and Adversity, Including Techniques for Processing Traumatic Memories, Building Resilience, and Finding Empowerment

Cathleen R. Barton

Overcome Trauma: A Comprehensive Guide to Understanding, Healing and Moving Forward from Past Trauma and Adversity, Including Techniques for Processing Traumatic Memories, Building Resilience, and Finding Empowerment

Table of Contents

01: Introduction: Understanding Trauma and Its Impact

Trauma is a complex and multi-faceted phenomenon that can have a significant impact on an individual's physical, emotional, and mental well-being. It can manifest in a variety of ways, from physical injuries and illnesses to emotional and psychological distress. Understanding trauma and its impact is essential for addressing and treating the effects of traumatic experiences.

Trauma is defined as an event or series of events that threaten an individual's sense of safety, security, and well-being. It can be caused by a wide range of experiences, including physical and sexual abuse, neglect, natural disasters, war, terrorism, and accidents. Trauma can also result from witnessing or being a part of a traumatic event, such as a car crash or a mass shooting.

One of the key characteristics of trauma is that it can have a profound and long-lasting impact on an individual's emotional and mental well-being. Trauma can lead to a wide range of symptoms, including anxiety, depression, post-traumatic stress disorder (PTSD), and other emotional and behavioral disorders. These symptoms can be debilitating and can significantly interfere with an individual's ability to function in their daily life.

The impact of trauma can also be felt in the body, as trauma can lead to physical symptoms such as chronic pain, headaches, and gastrointestinal problems. Trauma can also contribute to the development of certain illnesses, such as heart disease, diabetes, and cancer.

Trauma can also have a significant impact on an individual's relationships and interactions with others. Trauma can lead to feelings of isolation, mistrust, and fear, which can make it difficult for an individual to form and maintain healthy relationships. Trauma can also lead to difficulties in communication and intimacy, which can further contribute to feelings of isolation and loneliness.

It is important to note that not everyone who experiences a traumatic event will develop symptoms of trauma. Factors such as an individual's coping mechanisms, support system, and overall resilience can play a role in determining the severity and duration of the impact of trauma.

Treatment for trauma is essential for addressing and managing the symptoms and effects of traumatic experiences. Treatment options can include therapy, medication, and other forms of support, such as support groups and self-care practices. It is important to work with a qualified professional to determine the best course of treatment for an individual's specific needs and circumstances.

In conclusion, trauma is a complex and multi-faceted phenomenon that can have a significant impact on an individual's physical, emotional, and mental well-being. Understanding trauma and its impact is essential for addressing and treating the effects of traumatic experiences. With proper treatment, individuals can learn to manage their symptoms and move towards a healthier and more fulfilling life.

It is also important to understand that trauma can be experienced differently by different individuals and groups. For example, marginalized and oppressed populations may be more likely to experience traumatic events and may also face additional barriers to accessing appropriate care. This highlights the importance of a culturally competent and trauma-informed approach to treating and supporting individuals who have experienced trauma.

Additionally, it is important to recognize that trauma can be intergenerational, meaning that the effects of trauma can be passed down through families and communities. This is particularly relevant in the case of historical trauma, such as the trauma experienced by Indigenous communities as a result of colonization and forced assimilation. Understanding the role of intergenerational trauma can be important in addressing and treating the effects of trauma.

In working with individuals who have experienced trauma, it is important to approach them with empathy, understanding, and non-judgment. Trauma can be a sensitive and difficult topic to discuss, and it is important to create a safe and supportive environment for individuals to share their experiences and feelings.

It is also important to recognize that healing from trauma is a process, and it may take time for an individual to fully recover. It is not a one-time event but a journey that requires patience, compassion and support.

In conclusion, understanding trauma and its impact is es-

01: INTRODUCTION: UNDERSTANDING TRAUMA AND ITS IMPACT

sential for effectively addressing and supporting individuals who have experienced traumatic events. This includes understanding the unique ways in which trauma can affect different individuals and groups, as well as the role of intergenerational trauma. It also includes approaching individuals with empathy, understanding, and a non-judgmental attitude, and recognizing that healing is a journey that requires patience and support.

02: The Trauma Response and Its Effects on the Mind and Body

Trauma is a powerful and often debilitating experience that can affect a person's mind and body in a number of ways. The trauma response is the set of physical and psychological reactions that occur in the aftermath of a traumatic event, and it can have a significant impact on a person's overall well-being.

The mind and body are closely connected, and trauma can affect both in a number of ways. Trauma can cause a range of psychological symptoms, such as anxiety, depression, and post-traumatic stress disorder (PTSD). These conditions can be difficult to cope with and can have a profound impact on a person's quality of life.

Trauma can also affect the body in a number of ways. For example, it can cause physical symptoms such as headaches, stomachaches, and muscle tension. These symptoms can be caused by the release of stress hormones, such as cortisol, in response to the traumatic event. Additionally, trauma can also lead to sleep disturbances, which can further contribute to physical and psychological symptoms.

02: THE TRAUMA RESPONSE AND ITS EFFECTS ON THE MIND AND BODY

The trauma response can also have long-term effects on a person's mind and body. For example, people who experience trauma may be more susceptible to developing chronic health conditions, such as heart disease or diabetes. This is because the stress response can have a negative impact on the body's immune system, making it more vulnerable to illness.

Trauma can also have a significant impact on a person's relationships and social interactions. People who have experienced trauma may have difficulty trusting others, and may struggle to form close relationships. This can lead to feelings of isolation and loneliness, which can further contribute to mental health problems.

There are a number of treatments available for people who have experienced trauma. One of the most effective is cognitive-behavioral therapy (CBT), which can help people to understand and cope with the thoughts and feelings that are associated with the trauma. Other therapies, such as eye movement desensitization and reprocessing (EMDR) and prolonged exposure therapy (PE), can also be helpful in treating trauma.

Medication can also be used to help people cope with the symptoms of trauma. Antidepressant medications, such as selective serotonin reuptake inhibitors (SSRIs), can be effective in treating depression and anxiety. Other medications, such as benzodiazepines, can be used to help people cope with insomnia and other sleep disturbances.

In addition to these treatments, it is also important for people who have experienced trauma to take care of themselves in other ways. This can include getting enough sleep, eating a healthy diet, and engaging in regular physical activity. This can help to reduce the physical symptoms of trauma and can also improve overall well-being.

In conclusion, trauma is a powerful and often debilitating experience that can affect a person's mind and body in a number of ways. The trauma response is the set of physical and psychological reactions that occur in the aftermath of a traumatic event, and it can have a significant impact on a person's overall well-being. There are a number of treatments available for people who have experienced trauma, including cognitive-behavioral therapy, eye movement desensitization and reprocessing and prolonged exposure therapy, medication and self-care practices. It is important for people who have experienced trauma to seek professional help and support so that they can cope with the symptoms of trauma and improve their overall well-being.

It is also important for individuals who have experienced trauma to have a support system in place. This can include family, friends, and support groups. Having people to talk to and share their experiences with can be a valuable source of comfort and understanding.

Another important aspect of trauma recovery is addressing any unresolved issues or traumas from the past. Trauma often has a ripple effect, and unresolved past traumas can contribute to the development of new traumas. By addressing these past traumas and resolving them, individuals can reduce the likelihood of developing new traumas or experiencing a re-traumatization.

It is also important to note that the trauma response and recovery process are unique to each individual. Some people may recover more quickly than others and some may have more severe symptoms. It is important to understand that recovery is not a linear process and that individuals may experience setbacks or relapses.

In summary, the trauma response and its effects on the mind and body can be severe and long-lasting. However, with the right treatment and support, individuals can learn to cope with the symptoms of trauma and improve their overall well-being. It is important for individuals who have experienced trauma to seek professional help and support, to build a support system, and to address any unresolved issues or past traumas. It's also important to understand that recovery is a unique process and should not be rushed or expect it to follow a linear pattern.

03: Types of Trauma and Adversity

Trauma and adversity come in many forms and can have a profound impact on an individual's mental and physical well-being. Understanding the different types of trauma and adversity can help in recognizing and addressing the effects they can have on a person's life.

One of the most commonly discussed types of trauma is that which arises from physical or sexual abuse. This can include both childhood and adult experiences of abuse, as well as domestic violence and sexual assault. The effects of abuse can be long-lasting and include symptoms such as depression, anxiety, and post-traumatic stress disorder (PTSD).

Another type of trauma that is often discussed is that which arises from experiencing or witnessing a traumatic event. This can include events such as natural disasters, terrorist attacks, or mass shootings. The effects of these types of trauma can also include symptoms such as depression, anxiety, and PTSD.

A less well-known but equally impactful type of trauma is that which arises from neglect or abandonment. This can include childhood experiences of neglect or abandonment by parents or caregivers, as well as neglect in adult relationships. The effects of neglect can include feelings of worthlessness, abandonment, and trust issues.

Adversity can also come in the form of chronic stressors such as poverty, discrimination, or long-term illness. These types of adversity can have a cumulative effect, leading to a range of mental and physical health problems.

Another type of adversity is vicarious trauma, which occurs when an individual is exposed to trauma through their work or occupation, such as a first responder, medical professional, or therapist. This can lead to symptoms of PTSD and other mental health issues.

It is important to note that not all individuals who experience trauma or adversity will develop mental health problems. However, it is important to be aware of the potential effects and to provide support and resources to those who may be struggling.

Treatment for trauma and adversity can include therapy, medication, and support groups. It's important to find a treatment approach that works best for the individual, as recovery and healing are unique to each person.

In conclusion, trauma and adversity come in many forms and can have a significant impact on an individual's well-being. Recognizing the different types of trauma and adversity and understanding the potential effects can help in providing support and resources to those who may be struggling. It is also important to remember that recovery and healing are unique to each person, and that a range of treatment options is available to support individuals in their journey towards healing.

Another important type of trauma to consider is complex trauma. This type of trauma occurs as a result of prolonged and repeated experiences of abuse, neglect, or other forms of maltreatment. This can include experiences such as growing up in a war-torn region or living in a chronically abusive household. The effects of complex trauma can be far-reaching and can include symptoms such as dissociation, self-harm, and difficulty forming healthy relationships.

Another type of trauma that is becoming increasingly recognized is developmental trauma. This type of trauma occurs as a result of disruptions or failures in the development of the brain and nervous system, which can occur due to adverse experiences in early childhood. This can include experiences such as neglect, abuse, or exposure to violence. The effects of developmental trauma can include difficulties with regulation of emotions and behavior, as well as difficulties with attachment and relationships.

Trauma and adversity can also occur as a result of a traumatic loss, such as the death of a loved one or the loss of a limb. This type of trauma can be incredibly difficult to process and can lead to symptoms of depression and grief.

Lastly, it's important to recognize that trauma and adversity can also occur within the context of one's culture or community. This can include experiences such as discrimination, racism, or cultural dislocation. The effects of this type of trauma can include feelings of alienation, cultural confusion and identity issues.

In summary, trauma and adversity can take on many forms, and it's important to consider the unique experiences of each individual. While some types of trauma are more well-known and discussed, such as physical and sexual abuse, other forms of trauma, such as complex trauma, developmental trauma, cultural trauma and traumatic loss, are equally impactful and deserve attention and support. It's crucial to understand the different types of trauma and adversity so that individuals can receive the appropriate support and resources to promote healing and recovery.

04: The Trauma Healing Process: Understanding the Stages of Recovery

Trauma is a deeply distressing or disturbing event that can have a lasting impact on an individual's mental, emotional, and physical well-being. The trauma healing process is a journey that can take time and requires patience, understanding, and support. It is important to understand that everyone's experience of trauma is unique and their healing journey will be different. However, there are some general stages of recovery that are commonly recognized in the trauma healing process.

The first stage of the trauma healing process is the acute stage. This stage is characterized by feelings of shock, disbelief, and numbness. The individual may have difficulty processing what has happened and may have trouble sleeping, eating, or engaging in daily activities. They may also experience physical symptoms such as headaches, muscle tension, and fatigue.

The second stage of the trauma healing process is the denial stage. This stage is characterized by a refusal to acknowledge or accept the reality of the trauma. The individual may try to deny that the trauma occurred or may minimize the impact it has had on their life. They may also try to avoid thinking or talking about the trauma.

The third stage of the trauma healing process is the anger stage. This stage is characterized by feelings of anger, resentment, and frustration. The individual may be angry at themselves, the perpetrator, or others who were involved in the trauma. They may also feel that the trauma is unfair or unjust.

The fourth stage of the trauma healing process is the bargaining stage. This stage is characterized by a feeling of helplessness and a desire to regain control. The individual may try to make deals with themselves or with a higher power in an attempt to undo or change the trauma. They may also try to find meaning in the trauma by searching for a lesson to be learned.

The fifth stage of the trauma healing process is the depression stage. This stage is characterized by feelings of sadness, hopelessness, and despair. The individual may have difficulty finding pleasure in things they used to enjoy and may have trouble sleeping or eating. They may also feel guilty, ashamed, or responsible for the trauma.

The sixth stage of the trauma healing process is the acceptance stage. This stage is characterized by a recognition and acceptance of the reality of the trauma. The individual may have a renewed sense of hope and may begin to move forward in their life. They may also begin to find new ways to cope with the trauma and to find meaning in their experience.

It's important to note that these stages are not linear, and a person may revisit different stages at different times or may not go through all of the stages. Additionally, some people may experience long-term psychological symptoms, such as post-traumatic stress disorder (PTSD) and may need additional support and treatment. It's also important to note that healing is a unique and personal process that may take different form for each individual.

In conclusion, the trauma healing process is a journey that can take time and requires patience, understanding, and support. It is important to understand that everyone's experience of trauma is unique and their healing journey will

be different. However, by understanding the stages of recovery, it can help individuals better understand their own
healing journey and provide them with the support they
need to move forward. It's also important to seek professional help if needed and never feel ashamed to reach out
for support.

It's also important to note that the trauma healing process
can be different for different individuals. Some people may
find traditional therapy, such as cognitive-behavioral therapy, to be helpful in their healing journey. Others may find
alternative therapies, such as art therapy or mindfulness-
based practices, to be more beneficial. It's important for individuals to explore different options and find what works
best for them.

Another important aspect of the trauma healing process is
self-care. Taking care of oneself physically, emotionally, and
mentally is crucial in the healing process. This may include
things such as exercise, healthy eating, getting enough
sleep, and engaging in activities that bring joy and relaxation. It's also important to practice self-compassion and be
kind to oneself during this journey.

04: THE TRAUMA HEALING PROCESS: UNDERSTAND-
ING THE STAGES OF RECOVERY

It's important to remember that healing from trauma is not a one-time event. It's a continuous process that may take time, and individuals may experience setbacks along the way. It's important to be patient with oneself and to recognize that healing is not a linear process. It's also important to understand that healing is not the same as forgetting or erasing the trauma. It's about learning to live with the trauma and finding ways to cope with it.

In addition to individual therapy and self-care, support from friends, family, and loved ones is an important aspect of the trauma healing process. Having people to talk to and share the journey with can be incredibly helpful. It's also important for loved ones to be patient and understanding during the healing process, as well as educate themselves about trauma and its effects.

In conclusion, the trauma healing process is a journey that takes time, patience, and support. It's important to understand that everyone's experience of trauma is unique and their healing journey will be different. However, by understanding the stages of recovery, exploring different therapy options, practicing self-care and having a support system, individuals can find ways to heal and move forward in their lives. Remember that healing is not a one-time event, it's an ongoing process and it's important to be kind to yourself and to seek help if needed.

05: The Importance of Self-Care in Trauma Recovery

Self-care is a critical component of the healing process for individuals who have experienced trauma. Trauma can take many forms, from physical abuse to emotional neglect, and can have a profound impact on an individual's mental and physical well-being. The effects of trauma can be long-lasting and can manifest in a variety of ways, including depression, anxiety, and post-traumatic stress disorder (PTSD).

Self-care is a way for individuals to take control of their own healing and to actively work towards recovery. It involves engaging in activities that promote physical and mental well-being, such as exercise, healthy eating, and stress-management techniques. It also includes taking time for oneself, setting boundaries, and learning to say no to demands that may be overwhelming.

One of the most important aspects of self-care is understanding and acknowledging the impact of trauma on one's life. This means being honest with oneself about the ways in which trauma has affected one's thoughts, feelings, and behaviors. It also means acknowledging the impact of trauma on relationships and recognizing the need for support from others.

Self-care also involves learning to cope with the symptoms of trauma, such as flashbacks and nightmares. This can be done through a variety of methods, such as cognitive-behavioral therapy, mindfulness techniques, and medication. In addition, self-care includes taking steps to manage stress and to build resilience, such as exercise, yoga, and meditation.

Self-care also involves learning to set boundaries and to take time for oneself. This means saying no to demands that may be overwhelming and setting limits on the amount of time and energy one is willing to give to others. It also means learning to set boundaries with oneself, such as setting realistic goals and taking time to rest and relax.

Self-care also involves taking care of one's physical health. This includes getting enough sleep, eating a healthy diet, and engaging in regular physical activity. It also means paying attention to physical symptoms that may be related to trauma and seeking medical attention when necessary.

Finally, self-care involves reaching out for help and support when needed. This may include talking to a therapist or counselor, joining a support group, or talking to friends and family. It is important to remember that healing from trauma is a process and that it is not something that can be done alone.

In conclusion, self-care is an essential component of trauma recovery. It involves taking control of one's own healing, acknowledging the impact of trauma, learning to cope with symptoms, setting boundaries, taking care of one's physical health, and reaching out for help and support. It is a ongoing process of self-discovery and self-care that is essential for individuals who have experienced trauma to live a fulfilling life.

Self-care is not a one-time event, but a continuous process that requires ongoing effort and commitment. It is important to remember that healing from trauma is not a linear process and that there will be setbacks and challenges along the way. It is important to be patient with oneself and to recognize that progress may be slow.

It is also important to recognize that self-care is not just about taking care of oneself, but also about understanding

and addressing the societal and cultural factors that contribute to trauma. For example, recognizing and addressing
the impact of racism, poverty, and discrimination on mental
health and well-being is an important aspect of self-care for
marginalized communities.

In order to practice self-care, it is important to make a plan
and to set achievable goals. This may include setting aside
time each day for self-care activities, such as exercise or
meditation, or setting a goal to attend a certain number of
therapy sessions each month. It may also include making a
list of self-care activities that are enjoyable and meaningful,
such as reading a book or taking a relaxing bath.

It is also important to be mindful of self-care practices that
may be harmful or unproductive, such as substance abuse
or avoiding responsibilities. These practices may provide
temporary relief, but they ultimately perpetuate the negative effects of trauma and can lead to further harm in the
long run.

In addition, self-care also includes seeking professional
help, such as counseling or therapy, when needed. A trained
therapist can help individuals understand and cope with the

effects of trauma, as well as provide tools and strategies for self-care and healing.

In conclusion, self-care is an essential aspect of the healing process for individuals who have experienced trauma. It involves acknowledging the impact of trauma, learning to cope with symptoms, setting boundaries, taking care of one's physical health, and reaching out for help and support. It is a ongoing process of self-discovery and self-care that requires patience, effort, and commitment. Additionally, it is important to recognize the societal and cultural factors that contribute to trauma and to address them. Remember that healing is a journey, and it is not something that can be rushed or forced, but rather it is something that one should take the time to nurture and care for.

06: Processing Traumatic Memories: Techniques and Strategies

Traumatic memories can have a significant impact on an individual's mental health and well-being. These memories are often vivid, distressing, and can be triggered by seemingly insignificant cues in the individual's environment. Processing traumatic memories is an essential step in healing and moving forward. In this chapter, we will discuss techniques and strategies for processing traumatic memories.

One of the most effective techniques for processing traumatic memories is cognitive-behavioral therapy (CBT). CBT is a form of psychotherapy that focuses on the relationship between thoughts, feelings, and behaviors. The goal of CBT is to help individuals identify and change negative thought patterns and beliefs that may be preventing them from moving on from their traumatic experiences.

One technique used in CBT is exposure therapy. Exposure therapy involves gradually confronting the traumatic memories in a controlled and safe environment. The individual will be asked to describe their traumatic memory in detail, including their thoughts and feelings at the time. The

therapist will then help the individual challenge any negative thoughts and beliefs that may be associated with the
memory. Over time, as the individual becomes more comfortable with the memory, they will be able to think about it
without feeling overwhelmed.

Another technique used in CBT is cognitive restructuring.
This technique involves identifying and challenging negative thoughts and beliefs associated with the traumatic
memory. The individual will be asked to identify their auto-
matic thoughts and beliefs and to challenge them with more
realistic and balanced thoughts. This can help the individual
to see the traumatic event in a different light and to develop
a more positive perspective.

A different strategy is Eye Movement Desensitization and
Reprocessing (EMDR). EMDR is a form of psychotherapy
that uses bilateral stimulation, such as eye movements, to
process traumatic memories. The therapist will guide the
individual to recall their traumatic memory while engaging
in the bilateral stimulation. The theory is that the bilateral
stimulation helps to process the traumatic memory, making
it less distressing.

Another strategy is Mindfulness-based therapy. Mindful-ness-based therapy involves learning to be present in the moment and to focus on one's thoughts and feelings without judgment. This can help individuals to become more aware of their thoughts and feelings and to develop a sense of acceptance and understanding. Mindfulness-based therapy can be used in conjunction with other techniques to help individuals process traumatic memories.

Another strategy is Relaxation techniques. Relaxation tech-niques such as deep breathing, progressive muscle relaxa-tion, and visualization can help individuals to reduce their emotional distress and physical tension. Relaxation tech-niques can be used to help individuals calm down when they are feeling overwhelmed by traumatic memories.

It's important to note that processing traumatic memories can be a difficult and emotional process, and it's important to have a support system in place. This may include friends, family, or a therapist. It's also important to remember that healing is a process and it may take time.

In conclusion, processing traumatic memories is an import-ant step in healing and moving forward. There are various

06: PROCESSING TRAUMATIC MEMORIES: TECHNIQUES AND STRATEGIES

techniques and strategies that can be used to help individuals process traumatic memories, including cognitive-behavioral therapy, exposure therapy, cognitive restructuring, Eye Movement Desensitization and Reprocessing, mindfulness-based therapy and relaxation techniques. It's important to work with a therapist or counselor and to have a support system in place while processing traumatic memories. Remember to be patient and compassionate with yourself as healing can take time.

Another strategy for processing traumatic memories is to use creative outlets such as art, writing, or music. These outlets can provide a way for individuals to express their thoughts and feelings about their traumatic experiences without the need for words. This can be especially helpful for individuals who may have difficulty verbalizing their thoughts and feelings.

Art therapy, for example, is a form of therapy that uses art materials such as paint, clay, or collage to help individuals express their thoughts and feelings. The therapist will guide the individual to create art that represents their traumatic experience, and will then help the individual to explore their thoughts and feelings about the art.

Writing therapy, also known as journaling, is a form of therapy that involves writing about one's thoughts and feelings. The therapist will guide the individual to write about their traumatic experience, and will then help the individual to explore their thoughts and feelings about the experience.

Music therapy is a form of therapy that uses music to help individuals express their thoughts and feelings. The therapist will guide the individual to listen to music that represents their traumatic experience, and will then help the individual to explore their thoughts and feelings about the music.

It's important to note that these creative outlets should be used in conjunction with other techniques, such as cognitive-behavioral therapy or exposure therapy. They can be an additional tool to help individuals process their traumatic memories.

In addition to the above strategies, it's also important to take care of oneself while processing traumatic memories. This includes getting enough sleep, eating a healthy diet, and engaging in regular physical activity. These self-care practices can help to reduce stress and promote overall well-being.

In conclusion, processing traumatic memories is a difficult but necessary process in order to move forward and heal. There are various techniques and strategies that can be used to help individuals process traumatic memories, such as cognitive-behavioral therapy, exposure therapy, cognitive restructuring, Eye Movement Desensitization and Reprocessing, mindfulness-based therapy, relaxation techniques, and creative outlets such as art, writing, and music therapy. It's important to work with a therapist or counselor and to have a support system in place while processing traumatic memories. Additionally, self-care practices such as getting enough sleep, eating a healthy diet, and engaging in regular physical activity can also play an important role in promoting overall well-being. Remember to be patient and compassionate with yourself as healing can take time.

07: Building Resilience: How to Develop a Stronger Mind and Spirit

Building resilience is the ability to bounce back from adversity and to maintain a positive outlook in the face of difficult circumstances. It is a combination of mental, emotional, and physical strength that enables individuals to cope with stress and adversity, and to emerge from difficult situations stronger and more capable than before. Resilience is an important skill to develop, as it can help you to overcome challenges and to live a more fulfilling life.

There are several key strategies that you can use to develop resilience and to build a stronger mind and spirit. These strategies include:

– Setting realistic goals: Setting realistic goals is one of the most effective ways to build resilience. When you set goals that are achievable and that align with your values, you are more likely to feel motivated and energized by the process of working towards them. This can help you to maintain a positive outlook and to persevere through difficult times.

– Practicing mindfulness: Mindfulness is the practice of being present in the moment and paying attention to your thoughts, feelings, and sensations without judgment. It can help you to develop resilience by enabling you to stay focused on the present moment and to avoid getting bogged down by negative thoughts and emotions.

– Building a support network: Building a support network of friends, family, and professionals can help you to build resilience by providing you with a sense of connection and belonging. When you feel supported, you are more likely to feel confident and capable of facing challenges.

– Engaging in physical activity: Engaging in regular physical activity is one of the most effective ways to build resilience. Exercise releases endorphins, which are chemicals that can make you feel happier and more energized. Additionally, regular exercise can help to improve your overall physical health, which can in turn help to boost your mental and emotional well-being.

– Fostering a positive attitude: Fostering a positive attitude is one of the most effective ways to build resilience. When you focus on the good things in your life and practice gratitude, you are more likely to feel positive and optimistic about your future. Additionally, when you practice positive thinking, you can help to counteract the negative thoughts and emotions that can hold you back.

– Give back to community and help others: Giving back to community and helping others can help to build resilience by providing a sense of purpose and meaning. When you are able to make a positive impact on the world, you are more likely to feel fulfilled and satisfied with your life. Additionally, helping others can take the focus off of your own problems, which can help to reduce stress and anxiety.

In conclusion, building resilience is an ongoing process that requires time and effort, but the benefits are well worth it. By setting realistic goals, practicing mindfulness, building a support network, engaging in physical activity, fostering a positive attitude and giving back to community, you can develop a stronger mind and spirit that will help you to cope with stress and adversity, and to live a more fulfilling life. Remember that resilience is not about never experiencing difficulties, it's about being able to handle them and find the opportunities in them.

– Learning from failure: Failure is an inevitable part of life, and it is important to learn from it rather than dwelling on it. When you fail, it is important to take the time to reflect on what went wrong and what you can do differently next time. This can help you to build resilience by teaching you valuable lessons and helping you to grow as a person.

– Developing a growth mindset: Having a growth mindset means embracing challenges and seeing them as opportunities for growth. When you have a growth mindset, you are more likely to take risks and to view failure as a learning opportunity. This can help you to build resilience by teaching you to be more adaptable and to view challenges as opportunities for growth.

– Taking care of yourself: Taking care of yourself is crucial for building resilience. This means taking care of your physical, emotional and mental health. Eating a healthy diet, getting enough sleep, practicing self-care and managing stress are all important for maintaining good overall health.

– Seek professional help when needed: If you are struggling to build resilience on your own, it may be helpful to seek professional help. A therapist or counselor can help you to work through difficult emotions and to develop strategies for coping with stress and adversity. They can also help you to identify and address any underlying issues that may be contributing to your difficulties.

In conclusion, building resilience is a lifelong process that requires time and effort, but the benefits are well worth it. By setting realistic goals, practicing mindfulness, building a support network, engaging in physical activity, fostering a positive attitude, giving back to community, learning from failure, developing a growth mindset, taking care of yourself and seeking professional help when needed, you can develop a stronger mind and spirit that will help you to cope with stress and adversity, and to live a more fulfilling life. Remember that resilience is not about never experiencing difficulties, it's about being able to handle them and find the opportunities in them.

08: Finding Empowerment: How to Take Control of Your Trauma Narrative

Introduction

Trauma can be a devastating and debilitating experience, leaving those who have gone through it feeling lost, alone, and without control. However, it is possible to take control of your trauma narrative and find empowerment in the aftermath. This chapter will explore some of the ways you can take control of your trauma narrative, including understanding your trauma, facing your feelings, and finding support.

Understanding Your Trauma

The first step to taking control of your trauma narrative is to understand what trauma is and how it has affected you. Trauma is a deeply distressing or disturbing event that can have lasting effects on a person's mental, emotional, and physical well-being. It can be caused by a variety of events, such as physical or emotional abuse, sexual assault, natural disasters, or the loss of a loved one.

08: FINDING EMPOWERMENT: HOW TO TAKE CONTROL OF YOUR TRAUMA NARRATIVE

It is important to understand that everyone's experience of trauma is unique, and there is no "right" or "wrong" way to feel. You may feel a range of emotions, including anger, fear, guilt, and sadness. You may also experience physical symptoms such as headaches, fatigue, and difficulty sleeping. It is important to acknowledge and accept these feelings, rather than trying to push them away or ignore them.

Facing Your Feelings

Once you have a better understanding of your trauma and how it has affected you, it is important to face your feelings head-on. This may mean talking to a therapist or counselor, writing in a journal, or talking to a trusted friend or family member. It is important to find a way to express your feelings that feels safe and comfortable for you.

It is also important to remember that healing is a process, and it may take time. You may have setbacks, and that's okay. It's important to be patient with yourself and to remember that you are not alone in your journey.

Finding Support

08: FINDING EMPOWERMENT: HOW TO TAKE CONTROL OF YOUR TRAUMA NARRATIVE

One of the most important things you can do to take control of your trauma narrative is to find support. This can come in many forms, including therapy, counseling, support groups, or even online communities. It is important to find a support system that feels safe and comfortable for you.

It is also important to surround yourself with people who understand and support you. This may mean cutting ties with people who are not supportive or who may be triggering to you. It is important to remember that you deserve to be surrounded by people who care about you and want to help you heal.

Conclusion

Taking control of your trauma narrative can be a difficult and challenging process, but it is possible. By understanding your trauma, facing your feelings, and finding support, you can begin to take control of your story and find empowerment in the aftermath. Remember to be patient with yourself, and to surround yourself with people who care about you and want to help you heal. With time and support, you can come to a place of peace and acceptance.

08: FINDING EMPOWERMENT: HOW TO TAKE CONTROL OF YOUR TRAUMA NARRATIVE

Another important aspect of taking control of your trauma narrative is to learn how to manage and cope with the symptoms that may result from your trauma. This may include things like anxiety, depression, and flashbacks. It is important to educate yourself about these symptoms and to learn ways to manage them. This can include things like mindfulness techniques, cognitive-behavioral therapy, and medication. It is also important to find a support system that can help you manage your symptoms, whether that be a therapist, counselor, or support group.

Another important aspect of taking control of your trauma narrative is to find ways to take care of yourself. Self-care is crucial for healing, and it can include things like exercise, eating a healthy diet, getting enough sleep, and engaging in activities that you enjoy. It is also important to find ways to relax and de-stress, such as yoga, meditation, or listening to music.

In addition, it's important to be open to the idea of forgiveness, both for yourself and for others. Forgiveness is not about forgetting or excusing the hurt that was done, but it's about accepting that it happened, and not allowing it to continue to control you. It is a process and it can take time, but it is worth it in the end.

Finally, it is important to remember that you are not defined by your trauma. You are not a victim, you are a survivor. You have the strength and resilience to overcome what you have been through, and to live a fulfilling and meaningful life. You are capable of finding empowerment and taking control of your trauma narrative.

In conclusion, Finding empowerment after a traumatic event is a journey and it can be hard and take time, but it is important to understand your trauma, to face your feelings, to find support and to learn how to cope with the symptoms that may result from your trauma, to take care of yourself, to learn forgiveness, and to remember that you are not defined by your trauma. With time and support, you can come to a place of peace and acceptance and start to take control of your narrative and empower yourself.

09: Navigating Support Systems: Finding Help and Resources

Navigating Support Systems: Finding Help and Resources

When dealing with difficult situations, it can be overwhelming to try and find the right resources and support. Whether you are facing a personal crisis, dealing with mental health issues, or trying to navigate the healthcare system, it can be hard to know where to turn for help. In this chapter, we will explore some strategies for finding the support and resources you need to get through tough times.

First, it is important to understand that there is no one-size-fits-all solution when it comes to finding support. Different people may need different types of help and resources depending on their specific situation. However, there are some general tips and strategies that can be helpful when trying to find the right support for you.

One important strategy is to do your research. There are many different types of support and resources available, so it can be helpful to take the time to learn about the different options that are available. This can include things like therapy, support groups, and healthcare services. By researching different options, you can get a better sense of what might be the best fit for your needs.

Another important strategy is to reach out to people you trust. This can include friends, family members, and other loved ones who can provide you with emotional support and guidance. They may also be able to provide you with information about different resources and support systems that they have used in the past.

You can also seek out professional help. You can talk to a therapist, counselor, or other mental health professional who can provide you with guidance and support. They can help you work through your feelings and develop coping strategies that can help you get through difficult times. They can also help you navigate the healthcare system and find the right resources for your needs.

Additionally, many organizations, such as non-profits and government agencies, provide a wide range of services and support to those who need it. You can contact these organizations directly and ask about the services they offer. They can provide you with information about programs and services that may be able to help you.

09: NAVIGATING SUPPORT SYSTEMS: FINDING HELP AND RESOURCES

In addition, many communities have helplines that provide a wide range of support services and resources. They can provide you with information about local services and resources and connect you with the right people who can help.

It is also important to know your rights. This can include understanding your rights as a patient and your rights to access healthcare services and other types of support. Knowing your rights can help you advocate for yourself and get the help you need.

Finally, it is important to remember that you are not alone. There are many people who are going through similar situations and who have been able to find the support and resources they need to get through tough times. It may take some time and effort to find the right resources and support, but with persistence and determination, you can get the help you need.

In conclusion, finding the right support and resources can be a challenging task, but with the right strategies, you can navigate the support systems and find the help you need. It is important to do your research, reach out to people you trust, seek professional help, and know your rights. Remember that you are not alone and that with persistence, you can get the help you need to get through difficult times.

It's also important to be open to trying different types of support and resources. What works for one person may not work for another, so it's important to be willing to try different options and find what works best for you. This may include therapy, medication, support groups, and other types of resources.

Another important aspect of navigating support systems is being aware of cultural and language barriers. If English is not your first language, or if you come from a different cultural background, it may be difficult to find resources and support that are tailored to your specific needs. In this case, it may be helpful to seek out resources and support that are culturally and linguistically appropriate. This may include organizations that serve specific ethnic and linguistic communities or translation services that can help you communicate with healthcare providers and other types of support.

It's also important to be aware of financial barriers when seeking help and resources. Many support systems and resources require payment, and this can be a barrier for some people. If you are unable to afford the support or resources you need, it may be helpful to seek out organizations that provide financial assistance or programs that can help you pay for the support and resources you need.

Finally, it's important to remember that seeking help and resources is not a sign of weakness. It takes courage and strength to admit that you need help, and it's important to remember that everyone goes through difficult times and needs support. Seeking help and resources is a sign of resilience and the determination to improve your well-being.

In conclusion, navigating support systems can be a challenging task, but with the right strategies and information, you can find the help and resources you need to get through difficult times. It's important to do your research, reach out to people you trust, seek professional help, and know your rights. Remember to be open to trying different types of support, be aware of cultural and language barriers, and financial barriers, and remember that seeking help is a sign of strength and resilience.

10: Trauma and Relationships: How Trauma Can Affect Connections with Others

Trauma can have a profound impact on an individual's ability to form and maintain healthy relationships. Traumatic experiences, such as physical or emotional abuse, neglect, or exposure to violence, can disrupt the development of secure attachment patterns, affect the way a person sees themselves and others, and influence the way they cope with stress and negative emotions. As a result, trauma survivors may struggle to trust, communicate effectively, and form intimate connections with others.

One of the most significant ways that trauma can affect relationships is through the development of insecure attachment patterns. Secure attachment patterns develop when a child feels safe and secure in their relationship with their primary caregiver, and as a result, they learn to trust and rely on others. However, when a child experiences trauma, such as abuse or neglect, they may learn that the people they depend on for survival are not trustworthy or safe. As a result, they may develop insecure attachment patterns, such as avoidant or anxious attachment styles.

10: TRAUMA AND RELATIONSHIPS: HOW TRAUMA CAN AFFECT CONNECTIONS WITH OTHERS

Individuals with avoidant attachment styles tend to avoid intimacy and close relationships, often pushing people away to protect themselves from potential hurt or rejection. They may have difficulty trusting others and may struggle to form deep emotional connections. On the other hand, individuals with anxious attachment styles may crave intimacy and close relationships, but may struggle to trust others and may have difficulty setting healthy boundaries. They may also experience intense feelings of insecurity and fear of abandonment.

Trauma can also affect the way a person sees themselves and others. Trauma survivors may develop negative self-perceptions, such as feeling guilty, ashamed, or worthless. They may also struggle to trust their own perceptions and may doubt their ability to make healthy decisions. As a result, they may have difficulty setting healthy boundaries and may struggle to assert themselves in relationships.

Additionally, trauma can influence the way a person copes with stress and negative emotions. Trauma survivors may develop unhealthy coping mechanisms, such as substance abuse, self-harm, or avoidance. These coping mechanisms can interfere with the ability to form and maintain healthy relationships. For example, substance abuse can lead to problems with communication, trust, and intimacy, while avoidance can interfere with the ability to resolve conflicts and work through problems.

Furthermore, trauma can also lead to the development of certain mental health conditions, such as PTSD or depression, which can further affect relationships. Symptoms of PTSD, such as flashbacks and hypervigilance, can make it difficult for the person to relax and feel safe in close relationships. Depression can lead to feelings of worthlessness, hopelessness and lack of energy, making it hard for the person to engage in social interactions and maintain relationships.

It's important to note that trauma can affect different people in different ways and it's not possible to predict how someone will react to traumatic events. However, there are several ways to help individuals who have experienced trauma to build and maintain healthy relationships. One of the most effective ways is through therapy, such as cognitive-behavioral therapy, which can help individuals to identify and challenge negative thoughts and beliefs, develop healthy coping mechanisms, and improve communication skills.

Another effective way is through trauma-focused therapy, such as Eye Movement Desensitization and Reprocessing (EMDR) which aims to process and heal traumatic memories, so the person can live a life that is less affected by traumatic memories. Trauma-focused therapy can also help individuals to develop a sense of safety, trust, and connection with others.

It's important for the person's support system, family, and friends to be understanding and supportive of the person's healing process. It's also important for them to educate themselves about trauma and its effects on relationships, in order to provide the right kind of support.

In conclusion, trauma can have a significant impact on an individual's ability to form and maintain healthy relationships. Trauma survivors may struggle with trust, communication, and intimacy due to the development of insecure attachment patterns, negative self-perceptions, and unhealthy coping mechanisms. Additionally, trauma can also lead to the development of certain mental health conditions, such as PTSD or depression, which can further affect relationships.

However, there are ways to help individuals who have experienced trauma to build and maintain healthy relationships. Therapy, such as cognitive-behavioral therapy and trauma-focused therapy, can help individuals to identify and challenge negative thoughts and beliefs, develop healthy coping mechanisms, and improve communication skills. It's also important for the person's support system, family, and friends to be understanding and supportive of the person's healing process and educate themselves about trauma and its effects on relationships.

It's essential to remember that healing and recovery from trauma is a process and it takes time. It's important to be patient and compassionate with oneself and others who have experienced trauma, and to keep in mind that healing and forming healthy relationships is possible.

11: Trauma and Mental Health: Understanding the Connection

Trauma and mental health are closely connected, as experiences of trauma can have a profound impact on an individual's mental well-being. Trauma refers to a wide range of experiences, including physical and emotional abuse, neglect, natural disasters, and military combat. The effects of trauma can be long-lasting and can manifest in a variety of ways, including anxiety, depression, and post-traumatic stress disorder (PTSD).

When an individual experiences a traumatic event, their brain and body respond in a way that is designed to protect them from harm. The body's "fight or flight" response is activated, releasing hormones such as adrenaline and cortisol that help the individual respond to the threat. This response can be helpful in the immediate aftermath of a traumatic event, as it allows the individual to take action to protect themselves. However, if the trauma is not resolved, the individual may continue to experience the symptoms of this response, such as increased heart rate, difficulty sleeping, and difficulty concentrating.

For some individuals, the effects of trauma may not become

apparent until weeks, months, or even years after the event. This is particularly true for individuals who have experienced complex trauma, such as ongoing abuse or neglect. Complex trauma is characterized by repeated and prolonged exposure to traumatic events, and it can have a particularly devastating impact on an individual's mental health.

One of the most common mental health conditions associated with trauma is PTSD. This condition is characterized by a range of symptoms, including intrusive thoughts or memories of the traumatic event, avoidance of people, places, or activities that remind the individual of the trauma, and feelings of hypervigilance or increased arousal. Individuals with PTSD may also experience flashbacks or nightmares, and they may feel detached or emotionally numb.

Another common condition that can develop as a result of trauma is depression. Trauma can be a significant risk factor for the development of depression, and individuals who have experienced trauma may be more likely to experience feelings of hopelessness, helplessness, and worthlessness. They may also have difficulty sleeping, lose interest in activities that they once enjoyed, and have difficulty concentrating.

Anxiety disorders are also commonly associated with trauma. Trauma can cause individuals to feel constantly on edge, and they may experience physical symptoms such as a racing heart or difficulty breathing. They may also experience feelings of panic and fear, and they may avoid certain people, places, or activities that remind them of the trauma.

In addition to these specific mental health conditions, trauma can also impact an individual's overall well-being. Individuals who have experienced trauma may have difficulty trusting others, and they may have difficulty forming and maintaining healthy relationships. They may also have difficulty regulating their emotions, and they may experience feelings of shame or guilt.

It's important to note that not everyone who experiences trauma will develop mental health problems. Resilience and support from loved ones and mental health professionals can play a key role in helping individuals to cope with the effects of trauma. However, for many individuals, professional help is necessary to process and heal from the trauma.

Treatment for trauma-related mental health conditions typically involves talk therapy, such as cognitive-behavioral therapy (CBT) or eye movement desensitization and reprocessing (EMDR). These therapies can help individuals to process their traumatic experiences, learn to manage their symptoms, and develop coping strategies. Medications, such as antidepressants, may also be prescribed to help manage symptoms of depression and anxiety.

In conclusion, trauma and mental health are closely connected, and experiences of trauma can have a profound impact on an individual's mental well-being. Trauma can lead to a wide range of mental health problems, including PTSD, depression, and anxiety disorders. It's important to for individuals who have experienced trauma to receive professional help in order to process and heal from their experiences. Treatment for trauma-related mental health conditions typically involves talk therapy and medication, and can help individuals to manage their symptoms and develop coping strategies. It's also important for individuals, friends and families to understand the connection between trauma and mental health, in order to recognize the symptoms and seek help early on.

Additionally, it's important to address the societal and systemic issues that can lead to trauma, such as poverty, discrimination, and lack of access to resources. Addressing these issues can help to reduce the prevalence of trauma and improve mental health outcomes for individuals and communities.

It's important to remember that healing from trauma is a process, and it can take time. But with the right support and resources, individuals can learn to manage their symptoms and move forward in their lives. It's important to be patient with yourself and to seek help if you're struggling with the effects of trauma.

12: Trauma and Addiction: How Trauma Can Lead to Substance Abuse

Trauma and addiction are closely intertwined. Trauma can lead to substance abuse as a way of coping with overwhelming emotions and memories. Conversely, substance abuse can also lead to further trauma, creating a cycle that can be difficult to break. In this chapter, we will explore the relationship between trauma and addiction and how understanding this connection can aid in the treatment of both conditions.

Trauma is defined as a deeply distressing or disturbing experience that can have long-lasting effects on an individual's mental and physical well-being. Examples of trauma include experiencing or witnessing violence, natural disasters, sexual or physical abuse, and accidents. Trauma can also be cumulative, resulting from multiple small events that add up over time.

When an individual experiences trauma, it can have a profound impact on their mental and emotional state. They may experience symptoms such as anxiety, depression, and flashbacks, which can make it difficult to function in daily life. Trauma can also disrupt the body's stress response, leading to chronic physical symptoms such as headaches, chronic pain, and stomach problems.

Substance abuse, on the other hand, is the use of drugs or alcohol in a way that is harmful to the individual or those around them. This can include using a substance in a way that is not medically prescribed, using a substance for longer than intended, or using a substance despite knowing it is causing problems in their life. Substance abuse can lead to addiction, a chronic brain disease characterized by compulsive drug-seeking and use despite the harmful consequences.

The relationship between trauma and substance abuse is complex and multifaceted. Trauma can lead to substance abuse as a way of coping with the overwhelming emotions and memories associated with the traumatic event. Drugs and alcohol can provide temporary relief from these symptoms, leading the individual to use them more frequently and eventually becoming addicted.

Additionally, individuals who have experienced trauma are

more likely to develop substance abuse problems than those who have not. Studies have shown that individuals who have experienced traumatic events are at a higher risk of developing substance abuse problems, with the risk increasing with the number of traumatic events experienced.

Substance abuse can also lead to further trauma. For example, individuals who are under the influence of drugs or alcohol may be more likely to be involved in accidents or violent incidents. Additionally, individuals who are addicted to drugs or alcohol may experience financial, legal, and relationship problems, which can also be traumatic.

Understanding the relationship between trauma and addiction is crucial in treating both conditions. Trauma-informed care is an approach that recognizes the impact of trauma and incorporates this understanding into the treatment process. This approach recognizes that individuals who have experienced trauma may have different needs and may require a different approach than those who have not.

Treatment for substance abuse typically includes a combination of therapy and medication. Therapy can include cognitive-behavioral therapy, which helps individuals identify and change negative thought patterns and behaviors associated with substance abuse. Medication-assisted treatment (MAT) can also be effective in treating substance abuse, particularly for individuals addicted to opioids.

Trauma-specific therapies, such as eye movement desensitization and reprocessing (EMDR) or prolonged exposure therapy, can also be effective in treating the symptoms of trauma. These therapies help individuals process and make sense of the traumatic event, reducing the emotional impact and allowing them to move forward.

In conclusion, trauma and addiction are closely intertwined and understanding the relationship between the two can aid in the treatment of both conditions. Trauma can lead to substance abuse as a way of coping with overwhelming emotions and memories. Substance abuse can also lead to further trauma, creating a cycle that can be difficult to break. Trauma-informed care, which recognizes the impact of trauma and incorporates this understanding into the treatment process, is crucial in treating both trauma and addiction. It is important to address both conditions simultaneously, as one can exacerbate the other.

12: TRAUMA AND ADDICTION: HOW TRAUMA CAN LEAD TO SUBSTANCE ABUSE

It is also important to note that not all individuals who have experienced trauma will develop substance abuse problems, and not all individuals who struggle with substance abuse have a history of trauma. However, recognizing the potential connection between the two can aid in providing more comprehensive and effective treatment.

In addition to therapy and medication, other supportive measures such as self-care practices, mindfulness, and support groups can be beneficial in the treatment of trauma and addiction. A holistic approach that addresses physical, emotional, and social well-being can help individuals develop the skills and resilience to cope with difficult emotions and memories, and ultimately break the cycle of trauma and addiction.

It is important to remember that recovery from trauma and addiction is a journey, and it may take time for individuals to heal and recover. It is important to provide support and encouragement throughout the process and to remember that everyone's journey is unique. With the right approach and support, individuals can overcome the trauma and addiction and move forward towards a healthier and more ful-

12: TRAUMA AND ADDICTION: HOW TRAUMA CAN LEAD TO SUBSTANCE ABUSE

filling life.

13: Trauma and the Workplace: How Trauma Can Affect Your Career

Trauma is a deeply distressing or disturbing experience that can have a significant impact on an individual's mental and emotional well-being. Trauma can manifest in a variety of ways, including anxiety, depression, post-traumatic stress disorder (PTSD), and other mental health conditions. In this chapter, we will explore the ways in which trauma can affect an individual's career, including how it can impact job performance, relationships with colleagues and managers, and overall job satisfaction.

When an individual experiences trauma, it can affect their ability to focus and concentrate, making it difficult to complete tasks and meet deadlines. This can lead to decreased productivity and job performance, which can ultimately lead to disciplinary action or even termination. Additionally, trauma can cause individuals to struggle with maintaining healthy relationships with colleagues and managers, which can further impact their ability to succeed in their careers.

13: TRAUMA AND THE WORKPLACE: HOW TRAUMA CAN AFFECT YOUR CAREER

Trauma can also affect an individual's ability to cope with stress and handle difficult situations in the workplace. For example, an individual who has experienced trauma may struggle with handling criticism from a manager or dealing with a difficult customer. This can lead to increased absenteeism and high turnover rates, which can be detrimental to both the individual and the organization as a whole.

Furthermore, trauma can also affect an individual's ability to advance in their career. Those who have experienced trauma may struggle with networking, public speaking, and other important aspects of career development. This can make it difficult for individuals to secure promotions or move up in their organizations.

However, it is important to note that not all individuals who have experienced trauma will experience these negative effects in the workplace. Many people who have experienced trauma are able to successfully navigate their careers. Additionally, there are resources available to help individuals who are struggling with the effects of trauma in the workplace.

For example, employee assistance programs (EAPs) are

available to provide support and resources to employees who are struggling with mental health issues, including those related to trauma. These programs can provide counseling, therapy, and other forms of support to help employees cope with their experiences and improve their job performance.

Moreover, employers and managers can also play a role in supporting employees who have experienced trauma. This can include providing accommodations such as flexible schedules, additional time off, or changes to job duties. Additionally, managers and colleagues can be trained on how to recognize the signs of trauma and how to provide support to those who are struggling.

In conclusion, trauma can have a significant impact on an individual's career. It can affect job performance, relationships with colleagues and managers, and overall job satisfaction. However, with the right resources and support, individuals who have experienced trauma can successfully navigate their careers. Employers and managers can also play an important role in supporting employees who have experienced trauma and creating a more supportive and understanding work environment.

Another important aspect of addressing trauma in the workplace is creating a culture of openness and understanding. Many individuals who have experienced trauma may feel ashamed or embarrassed to talk about their experiences, which can further exacerbate the negative effects of trauma. By creating a culture where individuals feel safe and supported to talk about their experiences, employers and managers can help to mitigate the negative effects of trauma.

Additionally, employers can also provide training and education on trauma and its effects, for both employees and managers. This can help to increase understanding and awareness of the issue, and promote a more supportive and inclusive workplace.

It's also important to note that some individuals may require accommodations and support in order to function well in their jobs. These accommodations can include flexible work schedules, modified job duties, or additional time off for therapy and treatment. Employers should be willing to work with employees to provide these accommodations, as they can make a significant difference in helping individuals to manage the effects of trauma and be successful in their careers.

In summary, trauma can have a significant impact on an individual's career, but with the right resources and support, individuals can successfully navigate their careers. Employers and managers play an important role in creating a supportive and understanding work environment, and providing resources and support for employees who have experienced trauma. By creating a culture of openness and understanding, providing training and education, and offering accommodations, employers can help to mitigate the negative effects of trauma and promote a more inclusive and supportive workplace.

14: Trauma and the Legal System: Navigating the Challenges of Trauma and the Justice System

Trauma and the legal system can be a challenging and difficult topic to navigate. Trauma can affect individuals in a variety of ways and can have a significant impact on their ability to participate in the legal system. This chapter will explore the challenges of trauma and the justice system and provide strategies for navigating these challenges.

Trauma can be defined as a psychological response to a traumatic event or series of events. It can include symptoms such as anxiety, depression, and post-traumatic stress disorder (PTSD). Trauma can also affect an individual's cognitive abilities, including memory, attention, and decision-making. These symptoms can make it difficult for a person to participate in the legal system, particularly if they are a victim or witness in a criminal case.

Victims of trauma may have difficulty remembering details of the traumatic event or may be reluctant to talk about it. This can make it difficult for them to provide testimony in court or for prosecutors to build a strong case. Additionally,

14: TRAUMA AND THE LEGAL SYSTEM: NAVIGATING THE CHALLENGES OF TRAUMA AND THE JUSTICE SYSTEM

trauma can cause anxiety and distress, which can make it difficult for a victim to participate in court proceedings.

Trauma can also affect the way a person perceives and interprets events. This can make it difficult for them to understand legal proceedings and can also affect their ability to make decisions. For example, a victim of trauma may be hesitant to testify in court or may be unsure about whether to press charges against their abuser.

Trauma can also affect an individual's ability to participate in the legal system if they are a defendant in a criminal case. Trauma can affect an individual's decision-making and can also make it difficult for them to understand the legal proceedings. Additionally, trauma can cause anxiety and distress, which can make it difficult for a defendant to participate in court proceedings.

The criminal justice system can be a traumatic experience for victims, witnesses, and defendants. The legal process can be long and drawn out, and individuals may have to relive the traumatic event multiple times. Additionally, the criminal justice system can be a stressful and intimidating experience, particularly for individuals who have experienced trauma.

To navigate the challenges of trauma and the legal system, it is important to understand the impact of trauma and to work with professionals who are trained to support individuals who have experienced trauma. This can include working with therapists, counselors, and other mental health professionals.

Victims and witnesses of trauma may also benefit from advocacy services that provide support and guidance throughout the legal process. These services can help individuals understand the legal proceedings and can also provide emotional support. Additionally, victims and witnesses may benefit from participating in support groups or other forms of peer support.

For defendants who have experienced trauma, it is important to work with attorneys who are familiar with the impact of trauma and who can provide support and guidance throughout the legal process. Additionally, defendants may benefit from working with mental health professionals who can provide support and treatment for trauma.

It is also important for the legal system to take into account the impact of trauma when making decisions about criminal cases. This can include providing accommodations for victims and witnesses who have experienced trauma and taking into account the impact of trauma when determining sentences for defendants.

In conclusion, trauma and the legal system can be a challenging and difficult topic to navigate. Trauma can affect individuals in a variety of ways and can have a significant impact on their ability to participate in the legal system. To navigate these challenges, it is important to understand the impact of trauma and to work with professionals who are trained to support individuals who have experienced trauma. Additionally, it is important for the legal system to take into account the impact of trauma when making decisions about criminal cases.

Another important aspect to consider when navigating the challenges of trauma and the legal system is the role of trauma-informed practice. Trauma-informed practice in-

14: TRAUMA AND THE LEGAL SYSTEM: NAVIGATING THE CHALLENGES OF TRAUMA AND THE JUSTICE SYSTEM

volves understanding the impact of trauma on individuals and adapting the legal system to better serve those who have experienced trauma. This can include training for legal professionals on the effects of trauma, creating a more welcoming and understanding environment in courtrooms, and using language that is sensitive to the needs of trauma survivors.

Additionally, it is important for legal professionals to understand the intersectionality of trauma. Individuals who have experienced trauma may also have other marginalized identities, such as being a person of color or being a member of the LGBTQ+ community. These identities can compound the effects of trauma and can also affect an individual's experiences within the legal system. Therefore, it is important for legal professionals to be aware of and sensitive to the intersectionality of trauma.

Another key aspect of navigating the challenges of trauma and the legal system is understanding the role of restorative justice. Restorative justice is an approach to justice that focuses on repairing harm caused by crime and working with victims, offenders, and the community to find solutions that are fair and healing. This approach can be particularly beneficial for individuals who have experienced trauma, as it can provide them with a sense of empowerment and agency in the legal process.

In order to effectively navigate the challenges of trauma and the legal system, it is essential for individuals, legal professionals, and the legal system as a whole to work together. This includes understanding the impact of trauma, providing support and accommodations for individuals who have experienced trauma, and implementing trauma-informed practices within the legal system. Only by taking a holistic approach can we truly address the challenges of trauma and the legal system and ensure that justice is served for all.

In conclusion, trauma and the legal system can be a difficult and challenging topic to navigate. Trauma can have a significant impact on an individual's ability to participate in the legal system and can also affect the way in which legal decisions are made. To navigate these challenges, it is important for individuals, legal professionals, and the legal system as a whole to understand the impact of trauma and to implement trauma-informed practices. Additionally, a holistic approach that considers restorative justice and intersectionality of trauma is essential for providing a fair and healing justice system for all.

15: Trauma and the Impact on Children and Families

Trauma is an event or series of events that causes significant harm or distress to an individual or group of individuals. The effects of trauma can be long-lasting and have a profound impact on the mental and physical well-being of those affected. Children and families are particularly vulnerable to the effects of trauma, as they are often unable to understand or cope with the traumatic event.

Trauma can take many forms, including physical, emotional, and sexual abuse, neglect, natural disasters, and exposure to violence. Children and families who experience trauma may display a wide range of symptoms, including anxiety, depression, post-traumatic stress disorder (PTSD), and behavioral problems. These symptoms can have a significant impact on a child's ability to form healthy relationships, perform well in school, and function in other areas of life.

Children who have experienced trauma may have difficulty trusting others, feel detached or detached from their emotions, and experience flashbacks or nightmares related to the traumatic event. They may also exhibit aggressive or self-destructive behavior, such as fighting or substance abuse. These symptoms can be difficult to recognize and understand, and can be misinterpreted as disciplinary or behavioral issues rather than symptoms of trauma.

Families who have experienced trauma may also have difficulty functioning as a unit. Parents may struggle with their own mental health issues, including depression and PTSD, and may have difficulty providing the emotional support and stability that their children need. They may also have difficulty communicating with each other or with their children, which can further complicate the healing process.

It's important to recognize that trauma does not discriminate and can happen to anyone, regardless of race, socio-economic status, or other factors. It's also important to note that trauma can have a cumulative effect, meaning that even small traumas can add up over time and have a significant impact on a child's mental and emotional well-being.

Treatment for trauma can take many forms, including therapy, medication, and support groups. It's important to find a treatment that is tailored to the specific needs of the child and family. Trauma-focused cognitive behavioral therapy

(TF-CBT) is a form of therapy that has been shown to be effective in treating children and families who have experienced trauma. TF-CBT is a short-term, structured therapy that focuses on helping children and families understand and process their traumatic experiences, and learn new coping strategies to deal with the symptoms of trauma.

In addition to therapy, medication can also be an effective treatment for trauma-related symptoms, such as anxiety and depression. Medication should always be used in conjunction with therapy and should be prescribed by a qualified mental health professional.

Support groups can also be an important part of the healing process for children and families who have experienced trauma. Support groups provide a safe and supportive environment where children and families can share their experiences, learn from others, and receive support and encouragement.

It's important to remember that healing from trauma is a process and it can take time. Children and families may experience setbacks and may need to revisit certain topics or issues as they continue to heal. It's important to be patient and understanding, and to provide ongoing support and encouragement.

In conclusion, trauma can have a significant and lasting impact on children and families. It's important to recognize the symptoms of trauma and to provide appropriate treatment and support. With the right care and support, children and families can heal and move forward with their lives.

It's also important to remember that trauma does not only affect the individual who experienced it, but it also affects the entire family. Children and families often have to navigate the aftermath of trauma together, and it's essential to provide support and resources to the entire family unit.

Another important aspect of trauma is the recognition of its intergenerational effects. Trauma can be passed down from one generation to another, as parents who have experienced trauma may have difficulty providing a stable and safe environment for their children. This can lead to cycles of trauma and can make it harder for future generations to heal and move on from traumatic experiences.

Additionally, it's essential to understand that trauma can

have different effects on different people, even within the same family. Each person's experience and response to trauma are unique and should be acknowledged and respected.

Prevention is also an important aspect of addressing trauma. It's crucial to educate communities and families about the signs and effects of trauma, as well as providing resources and support to individuals and families who may be at risk of experiencing trauma.

In order to address the impact of trauma on children and families, it's essential to have a comprehensive approach that involves multiple sectors such as healthcare, education, social services, and criminal justice. Collaboration between these sectors is crucial in order to provide the appropriate support and resources for children and families affected by trauma.

In summary, trauma can have a lasting and profound impact on children and families. It's essential to recognize the symptoms of trauma, provide appropriate treatment and support, and address the intergenerational and systemic factors that contribute to the effects of trauma. By providing the necessary resources and support, children and families can heal and move forward with their lives.

16: Trauma and Spirituality: How Trauma Can Affect Faith and Beliefs

Trauma and spirituality are often intertwined, as individuals may turn to their faith or beliefs for comfort and understanding during difficult times. However, trauma can also have a profound impact on one's spirituality, potentially leading to feelings of betrayal, abandonment, and loss of meaning.

When an individual experiences trauma, they may question the belief that they previously held in a higher power or the concept of a benevolent universe. They may feel that their faith has been tested and found wanting, leading to feelings of anger and resentment towards their religion or belief system. Trauma can also lead to a loss of trust in the world and in others, making it difficult for an individual to connect with a higher power or find solace in spiritual practices.

Additionally, some individuals may feel that their faith or beliefs were responsible for their trauma, either through the actions of a religious leader or institution, or through the belief that they were being punished for their sins. This can lead to feelings of betrayal and abandonment, and may cause an individual to distance themselves from their faith or beliefs.

On the other hand, some individuals may find that their faith or beliefs provide them with a sense of strength and resilience during times of trauma. They may find comfort in the idea that their suffering has a greater purpose or that they are being tested in order to become a stronger person. They may also find solace in religious or spiritual practices, such as prayer, meditation, or connecting with a community of believers.

However, it's important to note that for some individuals, connecting with their faith or belief system may be challenging, and that's okay. Trauma can change us and our ways of thinking, and it's possible that an individual may find that they no longer identify with the religion or belief system they once held. It's important for individuals to allow themselves the space and time to process their experiences and to find meaning and purpose in their own way.

In summary, trauma can have a significant impact on an individual's spirituality, potentially leading to feelings of betrayal, abandonment, and loss of meaning. However, it's important to remember that different people have different ways of coping with trauma and finding meaning, and that it's important to respect and support an individual's unique journey.

It's also important for individuals who are struggling with the effects of trauma on their spirituality to seek out professional help. A therapist or counselor who is trained in trauma-informed care can provide support and guidance as an individual navigates the complex emotions and beliefs that may arise from their experiences. They can also help an individual develop coping strategies and resilience, and may provide referrals to support groups or other resources that can be beneficial.

Additionally, it can be helpful for individuals to explore other forms of spirituality or religion that may resonate with them more after experiencing trauma. For example, some individuals may find that nature-based spirituality or mindfulness practices provide a sense of peace and connection that traditional religions no longer do. It's important for individuals to explore different paths and find what works best for them.

It's also important to remember that healing from trauma is a process and it doesn't happen overnight. It may take time for an individual to come to terms with the trauma they have experienced and how it has affected their spirituality. It's important to be patient and compassionate with oneself and to take the time needed to heal.

In conclusion, trauma can have a significant impact on an individual's spirituality, but it's important to remember that healing is possible and that different paths may be taken to find meaning and purpose. It's essential to seek professional help, explore different spiritual practices, and be patient with oneself in the healing process. Remember that healing is a journey, not a destination, and that it's important to be gentle with oneself during this time.

17: Moving Forward: Finding Purpose and Meaning After Trauma

Trauma can be a devastating and life-altering event. It can leave us feeling lost, confused, and without a sense of purpose or direction. But it is important to remember that healing is possible, and that we can move forward and find meaning and purpose in our lives again.

The first step in moving forward after trauma is to acknowledge and accept that it has happened. Denying or suppressing the trauma will only prolong the healing process. It is important to give yourself time and space to grieve and process the emotions that come with the trauma. This may include seeking support from a therapist or counselor, or joining a support group for people who have experienced similar trauma.

Once you have begun to process the trauma, it is important to focus on self-care. This includes taking care of your physical, emotional, and mental well-being. Eating a healthy diet, getting enough sleep, and regular exercise can all help to promote healing. It is also important to find healthy ways to cope with stress and anxiety, such as through mindfulness practices like meditation or yoga.

17: MOVING FORWARD: FINDING PURPOSE AND MEANING AFTER TRAUMA

As you begin to heal, it is also important to find ways to integrate the trauma into your life. This may include finding meaning in the experience, such as by using it to help others who have experienced similar trauma. It may also involve finding a new sense of purpose or direction in life. This may involve returning to school or starting a new career, or simply finding ways to give back to your community.

Another important aspect of moving forward after trauma is to focus on building and maintaining positive relationships. Surrounding yourself with supportive and understanding people can provide much-needed emotional support and encouragement during this difficult time. It is also important to find ways to connect with others who have experienced similar trauma, as this can help to provide a sense of validation and understanding.

As you continue to heal and move forward, it is important to remember that healing is not a linear process. There may be setbacks and triggers that cause the trauma to feel fresh again. It is important to be patient with yourself and to understand that healing takes time. It is also important to remember that it is not necessary to achieve a state of complete healing in order to move forward and find purpose and meaning in life again.

In conclusion, moving forward after trauma can be a difficult and challenging process, but it is possible. By acknowledging and accepting the trauma, focusing on self-care, finding ways to integrate the trauma into your life, building positive relationships, and being patient with yourself, you can begin to heal and find purpose and meaning in your life again. Remember to reach out for help, be kind to yourself and don't give up hope.

It's important to know that healing is a personal journey, what works for one person may not work for another, so be open to explore different options and different paths. It's also important to remind yourself that trauma does not define you and you are capable of overcoming it and finding a new path in life.

Another important aspect of moving forward after trauma is to focus on the present and the future, rather than dwelling on the past. This may involve setting goals for yourself and working towards them, whether they are related to your career, personal relationships, or personal growth. By setting and achieving goals, you can begin to regain a sense of control over your life and a sense of purpose.

It may also be helpful to engage in activities that bring you joy and fulfillment. This can include hobbies, volunteer work, or other interests that you are passionate about. Engaging in activities that you enjoy can help to take your mind off of the trauma and provide a sense of accomplishment and satisfaction.

Another important aspect of moving forward after trauma is to focus on forgiveness. Forgiveness is not about forgetting or excusing the actions of the person or event that caused the trauma, but rather about letting go of the anger and resentment that can hold us back. Forgiving the person or event can help to release the emotional burden and move forward in a positive direction.

In addition, it's important to learn from the trauma and use it as an opportunity for personal growth. Trauma can be a powerful teacher that can help us to develop resilience, empathy, and a deeper understanding of ourselves and others. This can give us a new perspective on life and open up new opportunities for growth and self-discovery.

17: MOVING FORWARD: FINDING PURPOSE AND MEANING AFTER TRAUMA

Moving forward after trauma can be a difficult and challenging journey, but it is not impossible. With patience, self-care, and a focus on the present and future, it is possible to heal and find purpose and meaning in life again. Remember to reach out for help, be kind to yourself and don't give up hope.

It's important to remember that healing is not a destination, it's a process, and it's not a one-time event. It's a continuous journey that requires effort and commitment. You may stumble or fall down, but you can always get back up and keep moving forward.

In conclusion, Moving forward after trauma is a process that requires effort and commitment. By acknowledging and accepting the trauma, focusing on self-care, finding ways to integrate the trauma into your life, building positive relationships, setting goals and focusing on the present and future, forgiveness, and learning from the trauma, you can begin to heal and find purpose and meaning in your life again. Remember to reach out for help, be kind to yourself and don't give up hope.

18: Conclusion: The Importance of Continuing Support and Self-Discovery in Trauma Recovery

Trauma recovery is a lifelong process that requires ongoing support and self-discovery. The road to healing from trauma can be difficult and bumpy, but with the right support and resources, individuals can learn to manage their symptoms and live fulfilling lives.

The importance of continuing support in trauma recovery cannot be overstated. Trauma survivors often struggle with feelings of isolation and shame, and may not feel comfortable reaching out for help. It is crucial that they have access to a supportive community, whether that be in the form of therapy, support groups, or loved ones. Having a safe space to process and share their experiences can help individuals feel less alone and more understood.

In addition to ongoing support, self-discovery is also crucial in trauma recovery. Trauma can leave individuals feeling disconnected from themselves and their emotions. Through self-discovery, individuals can learn to understand and accept their experiences and emotions, rather than repressing or denying them. This can lead to greater self-awareness and self-compassion, which can help individuals build a more resilient and fulfilling life.

There are many different forms of therapy that can help individuals in their trauma recovery journey. Cognitive Behavioral Therapy (CBT) is one of the most widely-used evidence-based therapies and can help individuals learn to manage their symptoms and improve their overall well-being. Eye Movement Desensitization and Reprocessing (EMDR) is a therapy that can help individuals process traumatic memories and reduce symptoms of trauma such as anxiety, depression, and nightmares. Other therapies such as Mindfulness-Based Stress Reduction (MBSR) and yoga can also be beneficial for trauma recovery.

In addition to traditional therapy, alternative forms of healing such as art therapy, music therapy, and journaling can also be helpful for trauma survivors. These forms of therapy can provide individuals with a creative outlet for expressing their emotions, which can be especially beneficial for those who may not feel comfortable verbalizing their experiences.

18: CONCLUSION: THE IMPORTANCE OF CONTINUING SUPPORT AND SELF-DISCOVERY IN TRAUMA RECOVERY

It is important to note that trauma recovery is not always linear and individuals may experience setbacks. It is important to understand that healing is a process and it can take time. It is also important to note that everyone is different and there is no "one size fits all" approach to trauma recovery. Some individuals may find that traditional therapy works best for them, while others may find that alternative forms of healing are more beneficial.

In conclusion, trauma recovery is a lifelong process that requires ongoing support and self-discovery. Having access to a supportive community and various forms of therapy can help individuals manage their symptoms and improve their overall well-being. Remember that healing is a process and everyone is different, so it is important to find what works best for you.

It is also important for individuals to understand that healing from trauma is not just about managing symptoms, but also about learning to live a fulfilling life. This can involve setting and achieving personal goals, building healthy relationships, and finding a sense of purpose. Trauma recovery can also involve learning to accept and forgive oneself for

18: CONCLUSION: THE IMPORTANCE OF CONTINUING SUPPORT AND SELF-DISCOVERY IN TRAUMA RECOVERY

past experiences and mistakes, as well as learning to let go of negative thoughts and beliefs about oneself.

For some individuals, trauma recovery may also involve facing and addressing the root cause of their trauma. This may involve seeking justice for past injustices, such as filing a report or pressing charges against an abuser. It may also involve addressing systemic issues, such as advocating for policy changes or participating in activism.

It is also important to understand that trauma recovery is not just the responsibility of the individual. As a society, we must work to create a culture of understanding and support for trauma survivors. This includes educating ourselves about the effects of trauma, being aware of the signs of trauma in others, and being willing to offer help and support when needed. It also includes working to eliminate the root causes of trauma, such as poverty, racism, and discrimination.

In conclusion, trauma recovery is a lifelong process that requires ongoing support, self-discovery, and a commitment to living a fulfilling life. It is important to understand that

18: CONCLUSION: THE IMPORTANCE OF CONTINUING SUPPORT AND SELF-DISCOVERY IN TRAUMA RECOVERY

everyone's journey is unique, and it is essential to find the right forms of therapy and support that work best for the individual. As a society, we must also strive to create a culture of understanding and support for trauma survivors, and work towards eliminating the root causes of trauma. Remember that healing is possible and with the right support, individuals can learn to manage their symptoms, and live fulfilling lives.

Thank You

As we reach the end of this book, I want to say thanks for reading this book.

I want to get this information out to as many people as possible. If you found this book helpful, I would greatly appreciate you leaving me a review. This helps others find the book as well.

Disclaimer

This document is geared towards providing exact and reliable information in regards to the topic and issue covered. The publication is sold on the idea that the publisher is not required to render an accounting, officially permitted, or otherwise, qualified services. If advice is necessary, legal, financial, medical or professional, a practiced individual in the profession should be ordered.

This information is not presented by a financial or medical practitioner and is for entertainment, educational and informational purposes only. The content is not intended as a substitute for professional medical advice, diagnosis, or treatment. Always seek the advice of your physician or other qualified health care provider with any questions you may have regarding a medical condition. Never disregard professional medical advice or delay in seeking it because of something you have read.

The information provided herein is stated to be truthful and consistent, in that any liability, in terms of inattention or otherwise, by any usage or abuse of any policies, processes, or directions contained within is the solitary and utter responsibility of the recipient reader. Under no circumstances

DISCLAIMER

will any legal responsibility or blame be held against the
publisher for any reparation, damages, or monetary loss
due to the information herein, either directly or indirectly.